NOV 2 4 2003

find out about planes and helicopters

Written by
Sally Hewitt and Nicola Wright

Designed by
Chris Leishman

Illustrated by
Rachael O'Neill

Contents

Chrysalis Education

Flying

Planes can fly because they have engines and wings. Engines push the plane along the runway. Air rushes over the wings and lifts the plane into the air.

Cockpit

Tail

Turbo fan engines

Fuselage (body)

Wings

Undercarriage (landing wheels)

2

Helicopters do not need runways. Their engines drive rotors that spin and lift the helicopter straight up into the air.

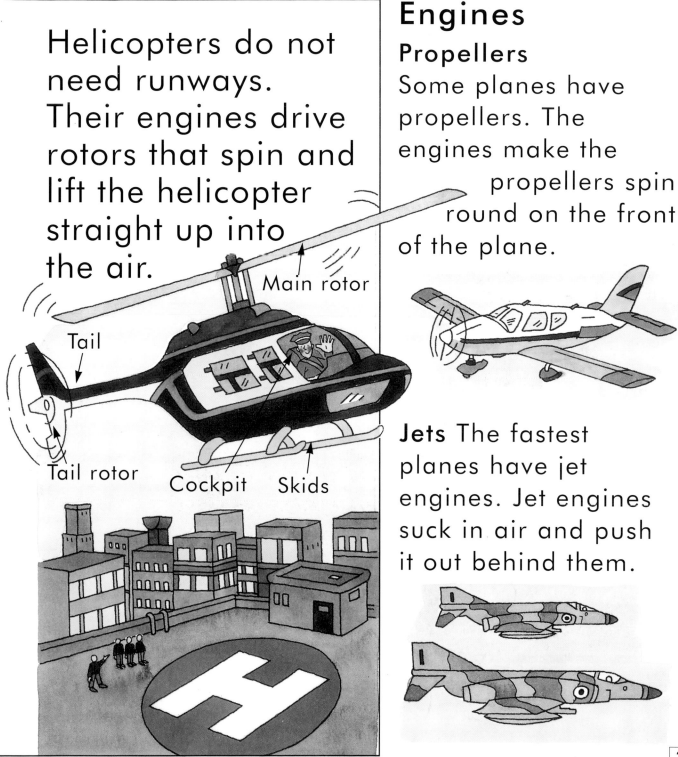

Tail

Main rotor

Tail rotor

Cockpit

Skids

Engines

Propellers

Some planes have propellers. The engines make the propellers spin round on the front of the plane.

Jets The fastest planes have jet engines. Jet engines suck in air and push it out behind them.

In the cockpit

The pilot controls the plane from the cockpit. In airliners, this is usually called the flight deck. Lots of screens and dials give the pilots all the information they need to fly the plane.

Microphone

Runway

Pilot (Captain)

> **Fun Fact**
> Airline pilots and co-pilots are given different meals. If the food makes one of them ill, the other can take over!

Earphones

Co-pilot

Special instruments

Control stick

The pilot moves the control stick backward, forward and sideways to control the plane.

Autopilot this is a computer that controls a plane in flight. Pilots control the take-off, but the autopilot can do most of the work during the flight, and even land the plane!

5

Airliners

Each year, millions of passengers are carried all over the world in airliners. The largest are jumbo jets that carry more than 500 passengers. Small airliners carry 20 to 30 people.

Cabin

Upper deck

Flight deck

British Aerospace Jetstream

Passengers

DC9

6

Boeing 747
(jumbo jet)

Tail plane

Tail

Hold

Engines

Fun Fact

The tail of a jumbo is as high as a six storey building.

Airliner shapes

Four engines Some airliners have four engines, two on each wing.

Three engines Some have three engines, one on each wing and one on the tail.

Two engines Some have two engines, on the wings or one either side of the tail.

Concorde

Concorde is the world's fastest airliner. It is supersonic, which means it flies faster than the speed of sound.

Streamlined shape

Passenger cabin

Delta-shaped wing

Concorde facts

Concorde has four engines and can fly at more than 2,000 km/h.

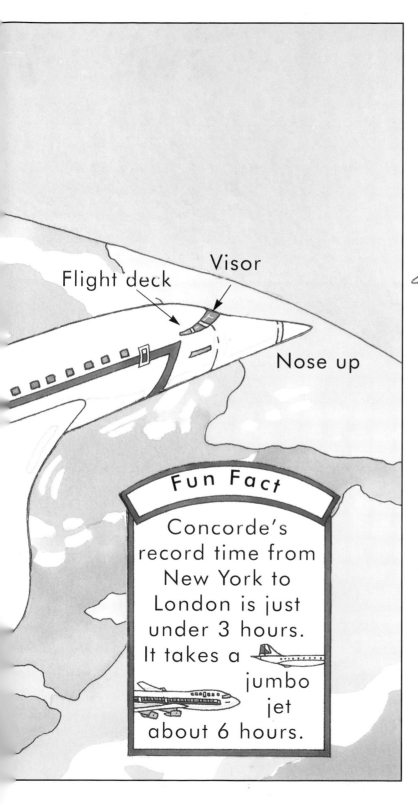

Flight deck

Visor

Nose up

Its visor and nose can be drooped down to let the pilot see the runway clearly.

Fun Fact

Concorde's record time from New York to London is just under 3 hours. It takes a jumbo jet about 6 hours.

When Concorde reaches the speed of sound, you can hear a double bang.

Special planes

Here are some unusual planes from around the world.

The Harrier jump jet can take off straight up into the air like a helicopter. Then it swivels its jet engines round and flies forward.

Floats

Seaplanes have floats instead of wheels. They can land on water.

Refueling

Small fighters cannot carry much fuel.

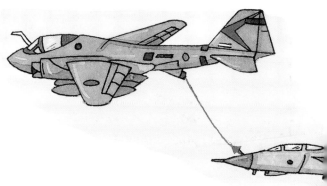

Jet engines

The Galaxy military plane is huge. It can carry heavy loads of tanks, trucks, and soldiers.

On long flights they refuel from special refuelling planes. The big plane has long pipes coming from its fuel tanks. The small plane fits a probe into a pipe and takes in fuel.

Aerobatics

Pilots control a plane's movement by changing the position of flaps on the tail and wings. Display teams, like these Red Arrows, can roll, loop, and spin their planes. This is called aerobatics.

Smoke trails

Single turbofan engine

Formation

Controlling

Pitch is the up and down movement. It is controlled by the elevator flaps.

Yaw is sideways movement. It is controlled by the rudder.

Bank or Roll Moving the ailerons on the wings makes a plane roll over.

 **Turning** is done by banking.

Small planes

Small planes can be fun for sport or they can do special kinds of work.

The tiny Pitts Special biplane was built to do extraordinary aerobatics.

Pitts Special

Microlight

Microlights are hang-gliders with engines. They are used for sport.

The bubble-shaped cockpit of the Optica gives pilots a clear view of the ground. It is used by some police forces.

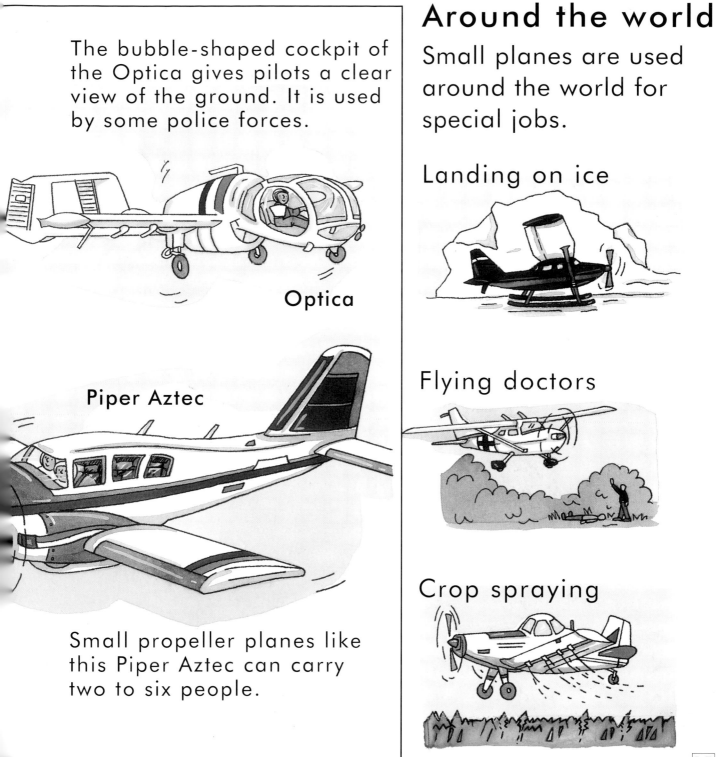

Optica

Piper Aztec

Small propeller planes like this Piper Aztec can carry two to six people.

Around the world

Small planes are used around the world for special jobs.

Landing on ice

Flying doctors

Crop spraying

Gliders

A glider has no engines to power it. An airplane, truck, or a winch has to tow it along until it is going fast enough to fly on its own.

Light body

Long narrow wings

The pilot releases the winch line when the glider is high in the air.

Winch line

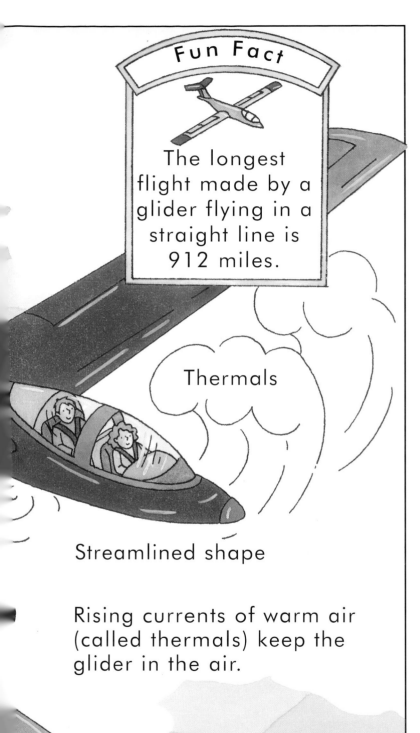

The longest flight made by a glider flying in a straight line is 912 miles.

Thermals

Streamlined shape

Rising currents of warm air (called thermals) keep the glider in the air.

Hang gliders

The pilot can be launched by being towed by a winch, or by running down a hillside.

The pilot is strapped in beneath the fabric wings. He or she uses a control bar and body movements to steer the glider.

Helicopters at work

Helicopters make good working machines because they can land and take off in very small spaces. They can also move up, down, backward, forward, sideways, and even hover in one place.

Passenger helicopters fly between airports, or take crew and supplies to oil platforms.

Movements

Up and down When the pilot tilts the rotor blade upward, the helicopter lifts into the air.

Forward and backward Tipping the rotor forward makes the helicopter fly forward . When the rotor is tipped back, it flies backward.

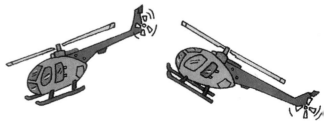

Tipping the rotor sideways makes it fly to the left or the right.

Fun Fact

The first helicopter flew in 1907. It lifted about 3 ft off the ground for about 20 seconds!

Search and rescue

Helicopters are very useful for search and rescue at sea.

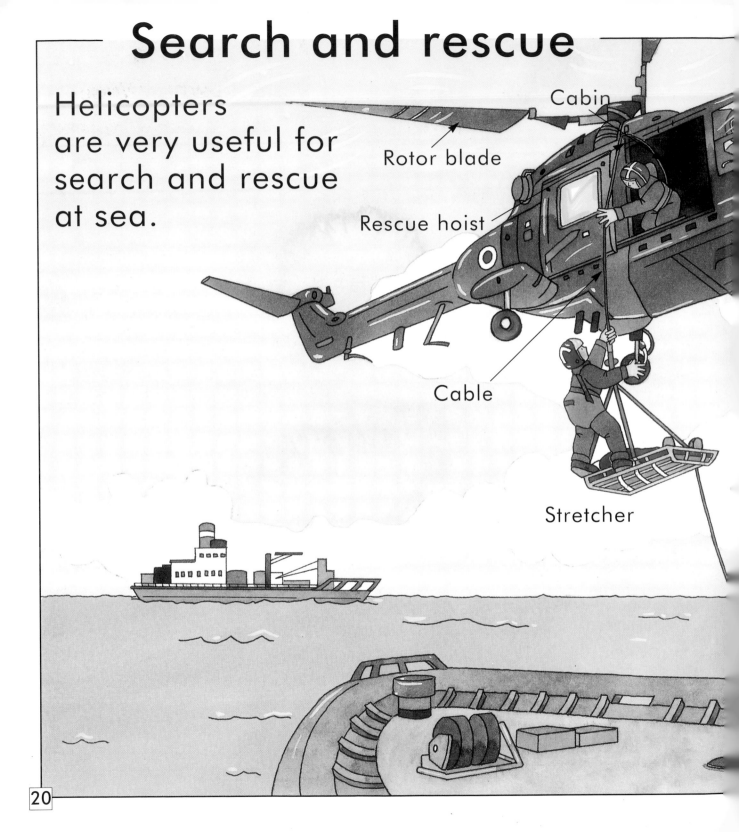

Cabin

Rotor blade

Rescue hoist

Cable

Stretcher

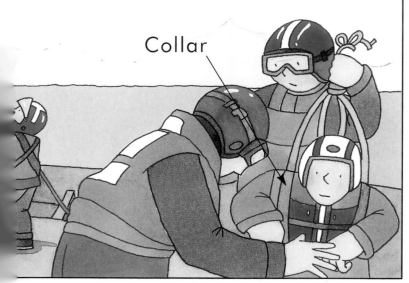

One crew member goes down on a cable and puts a special collar round the person being rescued. Then the cable is winched up into the helicopter with both people attached.

Collar

Special features

Helicopters with spotlights are used by the police.

Skycranes

Big, powerful helicopters are used as skycranes. They can lift and carry heavy loads to places that are very difficult to reach.

Sliding doors

Fun Fact

The largest helicopter ever built was the Mil Mi-12. It could lift the weight of nearly six elephants!

Cargo hook

Main wheels

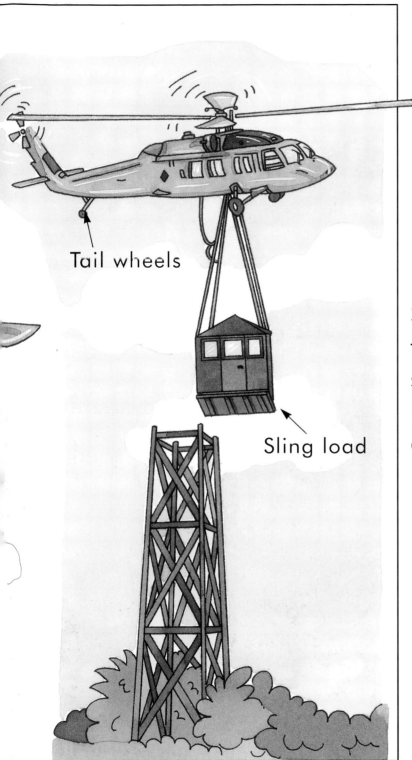

Tail wheels

Sling load

Special features

The Chinook helicopter has twin rotors that turn in opposite directions.

Safety The big rotors turn safely, high above people's heads.

Some helicopters have an opening in the cabin floor so the crew can watch the load below.

Index

Consultant: Captain Ian Evans
Editors: Nicola Wright & Dee Turner
Design Manager; Kate Buxton
Printed in China

ISBN 1 84238 654 5

10 9 8 7 6 5 4 3 2 1

This edition first published in 2003 by
Chrysalis Children's Books
The Chrysalis Building, Bramley Rd, London W10 6SP

Copyright © Chrysalis Books PLC